Soulful
MEDITATIONS

*Contemporary Parables
for Victorious Living*

Inspirational Devotional Study and Journal

Allen J. Shuler, Jr

Trilogy Christian Publishers
A Wholly Owned Subsidary of Trinity Broadcasting Network
2442 Michelle Drive
Tustin, CA 92780

For information, address Trilogy Christian Publishing
Rights Department, 2442 Michelle Drive, Tustin, Ca 92780.

Trilogy Christian Publishing/ TBN and colophon are trademarks of Trinity Broadcasting Network.

For information about special discounts for bulk purchases, please contact Trilogy Christian Publishing.

Manufactured in the United States of America

Trilogy Disclaimer: The views and content expressed in this book are those of the author and may not necessarily reflect the views and doctrine of Trilogy Christian Publishing or the Trinity Broadcasting Network.

10 9 8 7 6 5 4 3 2 1

Library of Congress Cataloging-in-Publication Data is available.
ISBN 000-0-0000-0000-0
ISBN 000-0-0000-0000-0 (ebook)

Dedication

To my loving wife,

Constance.

An anointed, beautiful, great woman of God, whose prayers, ideas, suggestions, and godly wisdom helped make this devotional a reality. I am so thankful God put us together. Many of the words in this devotional were inspired by your prayers and godly wisdom.

Acknowledgments

In addition to recognizing my beautiful and wonderful wife, Constance, I want to mention my thanks to God for our adult children: Takia, Dana (DJ), Jateria, Jasmin, Temperance, Morgan, Allen III, and our beloved grandchildren. My prayer is that you will fulfill your God-ordained purpose and continue

> *looking unto Jesus who is the author and finisher of our faith who for the joy that was set before Him, endured the crossing, despising the shame, and has sat down at the right hand of the throne of God.*
> **Hebrews 12:2 (KJV)**

Thanks also to my parents, Bishop Allen J. and Evangelist Sallie Shuler, who gave me the best inheritance anyone could receive: to know the Lord Jesus Christ, faithfully serve His Church, and love and uplift my neighbor.

I cannot thank everyone who has been a blessing in my life, but I am truly grateful for longtime friends and Christian leaders who have encouraged and labored with me in the gospel of Jesus Christ. Some of those to whom I would like to express my sincere thanks include Bishop Kevin & Lady Trudy Clark of Melchizedek Ministries; Rev. Richard & Sis. Deborah Williams; Pastor Steven

& Lady Lavetta Morgan of God's Harvest Community Church; Chaplain (BG) William Green (US Army); Chaplain (MAJ) Christopher Edwards (US Army Ret.); Pastor Earnest and Lady Keisha Bogard, III of Go Church Now; Pastor Stanley Moore of Progressive Baptist Church; CW3 Theardis Nelson (US Army Ret.); Bishop Harrell & Lady Gwen Browning of Faith Mission Ministries; Bishop Dr. Kevin & Lady Lorraine Betton of Cathedral of Praise; Pastor Lowell & Lady Phylliss Thomas of New Truway Church; Bishop William & Lady Naomi Martin of City of David; Rev. Farhley & Rev. Kathy Jones; Deacon Johnny B. & Sis. Lubertha Clemmons of Olivet Baptist Church; and Pastor Thomas DeWitt & Lady Naomi of First Baptist Church; and CPE educators Rev. David Turner and Rev. Dr. Larry Shostrom.

To you all, I pray God's continual blessings of love, joy, peace, and prosperity upon you, your families, and your ministries.

Table of Contents

Introduction

Greetings! First, giving all glory and honor to God the Father, Jesus Christ my Lord and Savior, and unto the communing presence of the Holy Spirit. As the Lord pressed upon my heart to share this devotional, Jesus reminded me how He spoke to His disciples and the people in parables. Reviewing Jesus' parables, we understand how Jesus' practical approach to teaching provided the audience with tangible stories that could connect their hearts and minds with the truth of God, the mission of the kingdom, thereby giving to all who receive Him by faith shall experience the glorious gift of salvation (Brown, 2012). It is from this viewpoint that I share these contemporary parables with our generation and to the generations to come. Through our life stories of challenges, failures, and victories, we can experience the transformational power and presence of Jesus' grace and unyielding love.

I hope and pray that you will break away from the busyness of life and take some time to read each soulful devotional as part of your personal or small group study. By thoroughly reading each lesson, digging deep into the biblical text, and exploring the questions, I believe this devotional will truly bless you. As you listen to what the Holy Spirit is speaking to your heart, journal your notes and relax your soul in the presence of the Lord. Yes, **R.E.L.AX.**:

R - remember God is with you;

E – exalt the Lord for His goodness in your life;

L – listen to the voice of God;

A – act upon what the Holy Spirit is leading you to do

X – express God's goodness through blessing & praying for others

I trust each parable will speak life to your heart and fill your soul with the joy, peace, and power of Jesus Christ. Lastly, I encourage you to continue studying the Word of God, the Bible and continue growing in the grace and knowledge of our Lord and Savior, Jesus Christ.

In Jesus' Amazing Grace,

Allen J. Shuler, Jr

By His Spirit

Not by power, not by might, but by My Spirit
says the Lord of host. **Zechariah 4:6 (NKJV)**

Have you ever noticed the power a balloon filled with your own air has compared to a balloon filled with helium? It's quite evident that the balloon filled with human oxygen barely floats across the room, but a balloon filled with helium has the power to travel miles down the road over many tall buildings.

God speaks to Zerubbabel in a vision and tells him that all He will do in Israel will not be done by human intellect or might but by the power of the Holy Spirit (Zechariah 4:6). We must take inventory of our lives and ask ourselves this question: what or who am I trying to change through my own natural power? If we are honest with ourselves, we'll realize that only God can transform the good, bad, ugly, and indifferent within our lives and turn things to work in our favor. We cannot do life in our own strength. We can only overcome sin, Satan, and the world by the power of the Holy Spirit.

Without the Holy Spirit working in our lives, we are just like a balloon filled with air from our lungs: we are going nowhere! But if we allow the Holy Spirit to have total control of our lives, we will rise and soar to our destiny!

Prayer: Dear God, help us acknowledge and allow the Holy Spirit to have full authority in our lives so we may accomplish the work You have called us too in the mighty name Jesus. Amen.

SOULFUL INSIGHTS FOR DAILY LIVING

1. The Holy Spirit empowers us to live a fulfilling Christ-centered life.
2. The Holy Spirit always works in agreement with the Word of God.
3. The Holy Spirit enables us to walk faithfully in the ways of the Lord.

BIBLE READINGS & STUDY QUESTIONS

1. What areas in your life are you trying to overcome by your own strength?
2. Are you allowing the Holy Spirit to lead you in the truth of God?
3. What did the Spirit of God reveal to Ezekiel? Read Ezekiel 37:1–14.
4. In Romans 8, Paul reveals what benefits believers have by living according to the Spirit?

JOURNAL

After reading the lesson text, take time and write down
what God is saying to your heart.

_____

_____

_____

_____

_____

_____

_____

_____

_____

_____

_____

_____

_____

_____

_____

_____

_____

_____

Do Good

And let us not grow weary of doing good, for in due season we will reap, if we do not give up. **Galatians 6:9 (ESV)**

Have you ever watched a hamster inside a cage running on the wheel? I mean, the hamster, with all its might, runs with a steady focus and intensity. Unknowingly to the hamster, he is not going anywhere. Well, life can be that way, especially when you give it your all, give it your best, and do it for good reasons. As believers, there are times in life when all we do for Christ appears to be like the hamster on the wheel.

Paul reminds the saints in Galatia that as they persevere in the faith, to maintain a life that remains faithful to God both spiritually and morally. Even when righteous living appears to be futile, Paul stresses, "do not be deceived, God is not mocked; for whatever a man sows, that he will also reap" (Galatians 6:7, NKJV). Like the notes of music that come together in a symphony, God will bring things together in your life at the appointed time (Schuller, 1995). With this in mind, we must hold fast to our godly convictions and keep sowing good seeds of righteousness at home with our family, with friends, and to our neighbors "for in due season we shall reap if do not give up" (Gal 6:9, ESV).

Prayer: Dear Lord, thank You for being a faithful rewarder of those who diligently seek You. Help us examine our hearts and do all we do for Your glory whereby sowing good seed in the earth that shall remain. Amen.

SOULFUL INSIGHTS FOR DAILY LIVING

1. Don't allow the struggles of life to hinder you from doing good.
2. Rely upon the Holy Spirit to empower you to fulfill your God-ordained assignment.
3. Don't give up now. Your blessing is nigh!

BIBLE READINGS & STUDY QUESTIONS

1. In Matthew 12:1–13, what did the Pharisees fail to see about Jesus doing good on the Sabbath?
2. In Psalm 37:3, 27–29, David highlights what blessings saints receive by doing good?
3. Who needs to know about you doing good? Read Matthew 6:1–4
4. What has stopped you from doing good for the glory of God?

JOURNAL

After reading the lesson text, take time and write down
what God is saying to your heart.

_____

_____

_____

_____

_____

_____

_____

_____

_____

_____

_____

_____

_____

_____

_____

_____

_____

_____

Build on the Rock

He is like a man building a house, who dug
deep and laid the foundation on the rock.
Luke 6:48 (NKJV)

One of the famous bedtime folk stories I enjoyed hearing and reading was the Three Little Pigs. In the story, three pigs are visited by a hungry wolf. The wolf came to the house of the first pig and threatened that he would huff and puff and blow down the pig's house. With a huff and a puff, the wolf blows down the pig's house because it was only built with straw. Afterward, the wolf visited the second little pig and presented the same warning that he would blow the house down. With stern confidence, the wolf huffed and puffed and blew down this pig's house too. Why? Because it was made of sticks. Full of pig stew and great confidence, the wolf ran to the house of the third little pig. The wolf proudly proclaimed, "little pig come out that house!" The little pig responded, "no, I will not come out!" The wolf quickly gave his warning that he would blow the pig's house down. So, the wolf huffed and puffed and blew, but the pig's house did not come down. Again, the wolf huffed and puffed and blew with all his might, but the house did not move. Finally, with all his might, the wolf took a great deep breath and fiercely blew upon the house; but the house did not make a shudder. Sighing in ultimate defeat, the wolf slowly wanders off into the woods. What was the difference? Why did this pig withstand the fierce winds of the enemy? Well, this pig withstood the wolf's wrath because his house was built on a solid foundation: Brick!

Jesus makes it clear to us that living without Him puts us at risk, just like the first two little pigs, of being destroyed by the storms of life or the schemes of Satan. On the other hand, those who follow Jesus and faithfully obey Him will be able to stand as the hymn goes, "on Christ the solid rock I stand, all other ground is sinking sand, all other ground is sinking sand" (Bradbury, 1864).

Prayer: Dear Lord Jesus, may we come to with an obedient spirit, not only to hear Your word but to be faithful doers of Your word. For in doing so, we shall be able to stand against tumultuous storms of life. Amen.

SOULFUL INSIGHTS FOR DAILY LIVING

1. Faith in Jesus gives our life an unshakeable foundation.
2. The Word of God: the *Holy Bible* is the blueprint

to building a rock-solid life.

3. Don't allow anyone or anything to persuade you to leave the solid rock: Jesus Christ.

4. Only in Jesus do we have the blessed assurance that we can survive life's storms.

BIBLE READINGS & STUDY QUESTIONS

1. After reading Luke 6:46–49, upon what spiritual foundation are you building your life?

2. Identify the areas in your life where you have built upon sand.

3. What are some of the consequences of being built upon sand?

4. What are you doing to ensure your life is built upon the rock?

JOURNAL

After reading the lesson text, take time and write down
what God is saying to your heart.

_____

_____

_____

_____

_____

_____

_____

_____

_____

_____

_____

_____

_____

_____

_____

_____

_____

_____

Accidental Blessing

But he handed Jesus over to their will.
Luke 23:25 (CSB)

While studying the colonies of staphylococci with his assistant Merlin Pryce, Sir Alexander Fleming accidentally stumbled upon a discovery that would greatly improve the medical wellbeing of humanity. Dr. Fleming's lab was small, and he mostly worked in disorderly conditions. Among the many Petri dishes that covered the room, Dr. Fleming noticed a particular culture that had been covered with mold (Maurois, 1963). He observed and realized the mold had dissolved the staphylococci bacteria. This coincidental discovery in Dr. Fleming's messy lab manifested a miracle mold that could kill off other harmful microbes. This accidental growth of mold turned out to be the basic form of penicillin, and since its discovery, millions upon millions of human lives have been saved from infectious diseases.

When we ponder on the events that led to Jesus' death, we cannot overlook the impact of Pilate's decision to give Jesus up to the ill will of the chief priests. Jesus was innocent, yet, they charge Him falsely and ordered He be given death. In his attempt to be cleared of this unjust trial, Pilate washed his hands and folded to the public pressure. As cruel as his decision was, Pilate didn't know the world, in its deprived state, needed Jesus, God-incarnate, the only begotten of the Father, to take that journey to Golgotha to pay our sin debt in full. For all who receive Jesus by faith would see that His accidental sentencing would ultimately serve to rid all humanity from the sickness of sin and provide a miracle antidote for our sinful soul. Jesus' crucifixion was truly an accident by Pilate and the Sanhedrin elders "for had they known, they would have not crucified the Lord of glory" (1 Corinthians 2:8, NKJV).

Prayer: Dear Lord Jesus, thank You for showing me that accidents serve to reveal God's glory in my life. Give me the strength to embrace every accident in my life with humble steadfastness. Amen

SOULFUL INSIGHTS FOR DAILY LIVING

1. Every situation in our lives works together for a greater purpose.
2. Although we may not understand why remember nothing *just happens.*
3. Amidst the chaos, there is a far greater glory yet to be revealed.

4. Praise God for every accidental blessing.

BIBLE READINGS & STUDY QUESTIONS

1. In Luke 8:44–56, what was the accidental blessing of Jairus' twelve years old daughter as it relates to the woman who had an issue of blood for twelve years?

2. What accidents in your life turn out to be your greatest blessings?

3. What have you learned from the accidental blessings in your life?

JOURNAL

After reading the lesson text, take time and write down
what God is saying to your heart.

_____

_____

_____

_____

_____

_____

_____

_____

_____

_____

_____

_____

_____

_____

_____

_____

_____

_____

Keep Your Lights On

Let your light so shine before men, that they may see your good works and glorify your Father in heaven. **Matthew 5:16 (NKJV)**

I recall times I would be invited to hang out with my friends, and when I got to the right street, I could not determine what house I needed to be at (please understand this was before we had Google Maps.) Why? Because the porch lights were off, and I could not see which house I needed to be at. After driving around for a few minutes, I would go to a phone booth and call my friend and ask him which was the right house, and he would tell me the house number and added I would see him standing on the porch with the light on. Quickly, I would return to my car and drive back to the designated street, and with no issues, I got to the house, and as promised, my friend was standing on the front porch by the light, signaling with his hands that I had made it to the right destination.

Jesus stresses that sinners can only know the right

destination as long as we, the disciples of Christ, keep our spiritual light on. As the younger generation says, Jesus is telling us to "stay lit" for the cause of the kingdom of God and let the world know that Jesus is the Way, the Truth, and the Life. No matter where we go or who we're with, every believer of Jesus Christ has the responsibility of letting the light of Christ shine before those who are lost in sin so they may know the way to experience the eternal, abundant life of Jesus Christ.

Prayer: Dear Lord Jesus, thank You for the opportunity to be bearers of Your light so those in darkness may come and know You as the Way, the Truth, and the Life. Amen.

SOULFUL INSIGHTS FOR DAILY LIVING

1. Don't be ashamed to let the light of Christ shine through you.
2. Keep your light on. The world needs to know the way to Jesus.
3. Remember God has given you His light to shine through the world's darkness.

BIBLE READINGS & STUDY QUESTIONS:

1. In Ephesians 5:1–14, what are the differences between walking in darkness and walking in the light?
2. Why is it so important for believers to keep walking

in the light of Christ?

3. What ways are you letting the light of Christ shine through your life to the world?

JOURNAL

After reading the lesson text, take time and write down
what God is saying to your heart.

_____

_____

_____

_____

_____

_____

_____

_____

_____

_____

_____

_____

_____

_____

_____

_____

_____

_____

_____

Rest

He makes me lie down in green pastures.
Psalm 23:2 (NKJV)

I often remember the times I stayed over at my grandmother's house as a child. My cousins and I would run and play through the neighborhood with the other kids. As lunchtime approached, my Grandmother, affectionally known as Big Momma, would come and stand on the front porch of her house and call us to come and eat lunch. Once we finished eating, Grandma would make us lie down and take a nap. With much resistance, we would complain about wanting to go outside to continue playing. Our decision was quickly overruled because Grandma was the juror and judge, so we had to lie down and take a nap. With her greater wisdom, Grandma would remind us that taking a nap was good for us.

David highlights his life as a shepherd who tended to his father's sheep. After taking the sheep on a long journey through the plains and hills outside of Jerusalem, David knew giving the sheep time to rest was good for their overall health. In the 21st century, we have filled every hour and second with some time of entertainment or work. We don't take time to step back, sit down, and rest awhile. We live in a world filled with twenty-four hours of unending drama and social unrest. Failure to turn off cell phones and the TV has led many people to suffer from social media depression and fatigue.

With a compassionate and loving heart, like my Big Momma, the Good Shepherd of our souls, Jesus Christ knows what is best for us. When we are overwhelmed with the busyness and struggles of life, Jesus divinely leads us to a place where He makes us sit down, rest, and He restores our soul with living water.

Prayer: Dear Lord Jesus, thank You for being the Good Shepherd who safely removes us from the cares of life and gives rest and restoration to our weary souls. Amen.

SOULFUL INSIGHTS FOR DAILY LIVING

1. Prepare for the journey ahead by embracing your seasons of rest.
2. Remember you cannot do everything, so know it's ok to just say "No!"
3. Remember proper rest and a good diet does your body much good!

BIBLE READINGS & STUDY QUESTIONS:

1. Why did God institute the Sabbath day? Read Exodus 20:8–1; Deuteronomy 5:12–14.

2. In what ways does Jesus reveal the purpose of the Sabbath? Read Matthew 12:1–13;

3. Mark 2:23–28; Luke 13:10–17

4. In Paul's letters to the churches, what else do we learn about living a life of faith in Jesus Christ as it pertains to the Sabbath? Read Colossians 2:1–17

5. What day is your Sabbath, a day of rest? Are you burning the candle at both ends?

JOURNAL

After reading the lesson text, take time and write down
what God is saying to your heart.

_____

_____

_____

_____

_____

_____

_____

_____

_____

_____

_____

_____

_____

_____

_____

_____

_____

_____

_____

_____

_____

Marinate

No one has ever seen God; if we love one another, God abides in us and his love is perfected in us. **1 John 4:12 (ESV)**

I'm not an avid cook, so I've learned from my wife that in order to have good tasting food, some dishes must abide in the seasoning. The longer the dish is in the seasoning, the more influence it will have over the plain taste of the food. Just putting the seasoning over the top of food does little to shift the natural flavor into a delightful taste that satisfies the palate.

The Apostle John, the brother of James, highlights in First John 4 that there is a difference between the Spirit of truth and the spirit of error. From this godly insight, whether in public or private, believers must be aware of the spirit in operation. John emphasizes that "every spirit that confesses Jesus Christ has come in the flesh is of God" (John 4:2, ESV). On the other hand, "every spirit that does not confess that Jesus Christ has come in the flesh is not of God" (John 4:3, NKJV). Greater still, because of Jesus' great love, John stresses that all who receive Christ overcomes the spirit of error.

John is not saying believers should leave those who wander in error, yet, he reminds the church that God has called us to be the seasoning in the earth. For as the agape love of God now abides in our hearts, we must manifest His love to the world. "By this everyone will know that you are my disciples, if you love one another" (John 13:35, NIV). So, in our journey to overcome the evil of this world, let us do so by the love of Christ. Just let it marinate!

Prayer: Dear Lord Jesus, thank You for being our guide who leads us to those who need You. Holy Spirit, empower us with Your strength and wisdom to be a positive influence in the lives of fellow neighbors. Amen.

SOULFUL INSIGHTS FOR DAILY LIVING

1. Seek out creative ways to share the good news of Jesus with other people.
2. Our greatest impact upon people is how well we live out the gospel of Jesus before them.
3. It only takes small acts of kindness to extend the love of Christ to others.

BIBLE READINGS & STUDY QUESTIONS

1. How can we marinate in a positive way to this present generation?

2. What hinders disciples of Christ from influencing the world?

3. Reviewing Paul's letter to the church in Corinth about love in 1 Corinthians 13 to John's account on love in 1 John 1–5, what are some key comparative insights that resonate from both texts?

JOURNAL

After reading the lesson text, take time and write down
what God is saying to your heart.

_____

_____

_____

_____

_____

_____

_____

_____

_____

_____

_____

_____

_____

_____

_____

_____

Broken but Not Forsaken

He heals the brokenhearted and bandages their wounds. **Psalm 147:3 (CSB)**

Some may remember the popular nursery rhyme written in the late eighteenth century called Humpty Dumpty. The rhyme in its mid-twentieth version states:

"Humpty Dumpty sat on a wall; Humpty Dumpty had a great fall; All the King's horses, And all the King's men, Couldn't put Humpty together again."

There is much debate as to what or to whom the rhyme referred. What is for certain, the character Humpty Dumpty fell, broke into pieces, and could not be put back together. What a tragedy! For a person to fall, to be broken, and left in ruin. This rhyme highlights a spiritual truth about humanity apart from God: fallen, broken, and many believe it is a world that has been forsaken.

In John 16:33, Jesus stresses to his disciples that

amidst the troubles they see and will face in the future, they are overcomers. Jesus' promise calls for us to trust Him and "Take Heart" (John 16:33, ESV)! Yes, this world is fallen, but we are not forsaken. Jesus can and still puts broken lives back together. In Jesus, we are given the power to transcend the fallenness of this world

> *We have this treasure in earthen vessels, to show that the transcendent power belongs to God and not to us. We are afflicted in every way, but not crushed; perplexed, but not driven to despair; persecuted, but not forsaken; struck down, but not destroyed; always carrying in the body the death of Jesus, so that the life of Jesus may also be manifested in our bodies.*
> **2 Corinthians 4:7–10 (RSV)**

What a blessed hope that Jesus can take our brokenness and give us wholeness. In the midst of chaos and sometimes cruel world, Jesus is the Christ who has the power to heal our brokenness and put us back together again. Take heart, my brother! Take heart, my sister! Jesus will put you back together!

Prayer: Dear Lord Jesus, thank You for healing the broken places in our lives. Help us to remember that we can cast all our cares upon You. Amen.

SOULFUL INSIGHTS FOR DAILY LIVING

1. Give Jesus access to heal the areas of brokenness

in your life.

2. Examine your life and release those things that keep wounding you to the Lord.

3. Some things in life can wound us deeply, so do not be afraid or ashamed to enroll and participate in a professional Christian care counseling ministry.

BIBLE READINGS & STUDY QUESTIONS

1. What broken areas in my life need Jesus' healing touch?

2. In Matthew 9:18–22; Mark 5:25–34; and Luke 8:41–48, what valuable insights do you grasp from the life of the woman who touches the hem of Jesus' garment?

3. What keeps you from trusting Jesus with your brokenness?

JOURNAL

After reading the parable take time and write down what God is saying to your heart.

_____

_____

_____

_____

_____

_____

_____

_____

_____

_____

_____

_____

_____

_____

_____

_____

_____

Build the Faith Muscle

So, then faith comes by hearing, and hearing by the word of God. **Romans 10:17 (NKJV)**

Most athletes would agree that playing successfully on gameday starts with practice. It is during practice sessions that plays are constantly rehearsed so each teammate will understand their assignment according to the coach's playbook. On a deeper note, most athletes understand that knowing the playbook is not enough. They must also condition and train their bodies in a way that gives them strength to endure grueling drills and practices and overcome the opposing team on gameday.

Paul shares with the church at Rome that all we know about God and His redeeming grace through His Son, Jesus Christ, is only made possible by believing in faith. Paul stresses that for us to understand the gospel, we must put our faith into action. Just like an athlete spends time in the gym to build natural muscle, Paul says to the church, the body of Christ, that building faith muscle requires we spend time in God's gym: His Word. Believing faith is increased by hearing the Word of God, thereby remaining open to the Spirit of God, and allowing His Word to workout in our hearts.

Prayer: Dear Lord Jesus, I believe Your report, that Your word is true about who You are; why You came, and why I need You. Lord, I receive Your word gladly into my heart so my faith will remain strengthened by and in You. Amen.

SOULFUL INSIGHTS FOR DAILY LIVING

1. Consistently, make time to read the Word of God.
2. Meditating and studying the Word of God helps us grow in the grace and knowledge of Jesus Christ.
3. Spending time in God's Word gives us the strength to stand against the schemes of the devil.

BIBLE READINGS & STUDY QUESTIONS

1. Why do believers fail to stand firm in faith?
2. What ways are you building your faith in Jesus?
3. In Matthew 4:1–11, what was Jesus' method of standing firm in the faith against the temptations of the devil?
4. In 2 Peter 1:1–11, what does Peter instructs us to add to our faith? Why?

JOURNAL

After reading the parable take time and write down what
God is saying to your heart.

_____

_____

_____

_____

_____

_____

_____

_____

_____

_____

_____

_____

_____

_____

_____

_____

_____

_____

_____

_____

Perseverance

Let us run with endurance the race that
lies before us, keeping our eyes on Jesus.
Hebrews 12:1–2 (CSB)

I am reminded of the famous story called *The Hare and the Tortoise* credited to Aesop, a Phrygian slave and storyteller believed to have lived during the sixth century BC (Jones, 2019). The tortoise becomes annoyed with the ongoing haughty attitude of the hare. Without giving it much thought, the tortoise challenges the hare to a race. Knowing he's the superior runner, the hare accepts the tortoise's challenge. They approach the starting line, the countdown is given, the race begins, and in an instant flash, the hare swiftly leaves the tortoise in the dust. The tortoise moves slowly along the route, inch by inch, step by step. It is quite clear that the hare has already won the race; however, the tortoise does not allow the hare's speedy start to deter him from pressing forward into the race. With the tortoise lost in his rearview, the hare stops and treats himself with a nap. After much time has passed, the hare jumps up from his nap and is warned that the tortoise is about to win the race. The hare takes off, and as he approaches the finish line, he sees the tortoise is inches away from winning the race. With all his might, the hare tries to overcome his mistake, but it is too late. The tortoise, with a steady focus, against overwhelming odds, perseveres and takes victory over the hare.

Paul's letter to the believers of his time endeavored to remind them to keep persevering in the faith. He reminds them of the heroes of faith: Abel, Enoch, Noah, Abraham, Sarah, Moses, and even Rahab; were all blessed because they endured to the end in faith without receiving the fulness of the promise; but God has provided us with something better through His Son, Jesus Christ (Hebrews 11:1–40). This gives us every reason to persevere like the tortoise, whereby we remain focused, looking unto Jesus, the author and finisher of our faith.

Prayer: Dear Lord Jesus, thank You for encouraging our hearts to persevere to the end. We can always trust in Your unyielding strength to help us finish the race that is set before us. Amen.

SOULFUL INSIGHTS FOR DAILY LIVING

1. Perseverance is a key component of faithful living whereby we deny ourselves, take up our cross, and daily follow Jesus.

2. Our life in Christ is not a sprint, but it is a journey

that we must endure until the end of the age.

3. Persevering in faith is only accomplished by living daily in Jesus' strength.

BIBLE READINGS & STUDY QUESTIONS:

1. Examining the life of the heroes of faith in Hebrews 11:1–40, how did they persevere in faith?

2. What is keeping you from persevering in the race of faith?

3. In Romans 5:1–5, what does perseverance produce in our life?

JOURNAL

After reading the parable take time and write down what God is saying to your heart.

_____

_____

_____

_____

_____

_____

_____

_____

_____

_____

_____

_____

_____

_____

_____

_____

_____

It Matters

The King will reply, 'Truly I tell you, whatever
you did for one of the least of these brothers
and sisters of mine, you did for me. **Matthew**
25:40 (NIV)

I am reminded of the reality TV series called
Undercover Boss. This short film series reveals the
outcome of company habits and flaws as one of the
high-ranking managers goes undercover to see how the
business is really going on the ground floor. The staff at
the entry-level have no clue that they are entertaining and
training a senior-level manager. While going through the
daily grind of the job, the undercover manager is quite
surprised to see and hear about the mistrust within the
staff and the ineffective policies and procedures that have
hindered the company from reaching its full potential.
After a few weeks of being exposed to daily interactions
of the job, the show's producers revealed the true identity
of the senior manager to the entry-level staff. With the
boss' identity now revealed, they honorably recognize
those who have really made a positive impact within the

company. The CEO now takes intentional steps to reward those who have done well and make needed improvements within their company business.

Jesus' message in Matthew 25 focuses on the consequences of decisions about five wise virgins and five foolish virgins, the giving of talents and the return on those talents, and the treatment of those of lesser status. Each account gives beneficial insights on several spiritual principles, but what stands in the middle of each story is an undercover boss who takes an interest in the way we prepare our lives, steward our talents, and treat those who are in distress or of meager means. What we do and how we do it matters to God. In every decision we make, Jesus the King of Kings, Lord of Lords, is the Eternal *undercover boss* who will reveal Himself on that great day and will say to us, "whatever you did for one of the least of these brothers and sisters of mine, you did for me" (Matt 25:40, NIV).

> **Prayer:** Dear Lord Jesus, help us to live a life being watchful, prayerful, and purposeful whereby we endeavor to make every opportunity to be a blessing to others. Amen.

SOULFUL INSIGHTS FOR DAILY LIVING

1. Living a blessed life in the Lord requires we live a life blessing other people.

2. The Christian life is not *all about you* but about

believers availing themselves to uplift the disenfranchised.

3. Intentionally look for opportunities to bless those who are in need.

BIBLE READINGS & STUDY QUESTIONS:

1. In Luke 12:13–15, what does Jesus stress about having abundance?

2. In the parable Jesus gives in Luke 12:16–21, what did the rich man fail to understand about his responsibility of having plenty?

3. What have you done lately for the least among us?

JOURNAL

After reading the parable take time and write down what God is saying to your heart.

_____

_____

_____

_____

_____

_____

_____

_____

_____

_____

_____

_____

_____

_____

_____

_____

_____

_____

Reppin the Kingdom

Now when they had seen Him, they made widely known the saying which was told them concerning this Child. **Luke 2:17 (NKJV)**

In the late '80s through the '90s, there was a rave among the youth and teens that took community love to a new extreme known as *reppin*. This perspective not only meant identifying with one's neighborhood, but it involved hand symbols, specific clothing colors, witty slang, as well as unwavering loyalty. Without any provoking, people made it clear that they were proud to be from certain parts of the city, e.g., central, eastside, northside, or the westside of town. *Reppin* was part of everything these young people did. No matter where they went, they made it widely known who they were and with whom they were.

In Luke 2, some shepherds are out on the plains tending to their sheep by night when suddenly they are visited by the angel of the Lord. This angel tells the shepherds not to be afraid and receive the good news about the Savior, Christ the Lord was born in Bethlehem. As the shepherds receive the word from the angel, they immediately go and find Mary and Joseph and the Babe lying in a manger. Upon seeing what the angels told them, the shepherds wasted no time *reppin* the good news about the Child to others.

Today, we, the body of Christ, must take hold of the shepherds' faith. It is not enough to hear the good news and see the miracles of God in our lives. We must take the next step and boldly rep what we have experienced. The shepherds not only received the Word of God. They took the journey to find Jesus, and when they saw Him, the shepherds went and shared their experiences with others. Likewise, we must not be ashamed to rep the good news about Jesus to this present world.

Prayer: Dear God, give us that same spiritual boldness as the shepherds. As we glorify and praise You for all we have seen, help us to use every moment to rep to the world the blessed opportunity of knowing the Savior, Jesus Christ the Lord. Amen.

SOULFUL INSIGHTS FOR DAILY LIVING

1. *Reppin* is not just about singing praises to God, but it requires telling the world about having a relationship with Him.

2. Living a life that faithfully glorifies and worships God is the best way to let the world know you are *reppin* Jesus.

3. Don't let fear nor rejection keep you from *reppin* Jesus before the world.

BIBLE READINGS & STUDY QUESTIONS

1. Reviewing Acts 1:4–8, why are believers filled with the Holy Spirit?

2. In 2 Corinthians 4:1–6, why does Paul rep the gospel of Jesus Christ?

3. When was the last time you repped the Kingdom?

4. What are some ways we can rep Jesus to others?

JOURNAL

After reading the parable take time and write down what God is saying to your heart.

_____

_____

_____

_____

_____

_____

_____

_____

_____

_____

_____

_____

_____

_____

_____

_____

_____

Afterword

Know Jesus, Receive Jesus, Live for Jesus

As you have journeyed through these lessons, I pray your heart was encouraged to keep following Jesus. I pray you also took time to journal what the Holy Spirit ministered to your heart. With so much negativity in the world today, many people are still wondering, does my life have a purpose. Yes, it does! God loves you! You are valuable to Him. He wants you to have an abundant soulful life! He expressed His love to us by sending us His very best gift, His only begotten Son, Jesus Christ. Jesus came not just for the world, but He came specifically for you and me. Jesus desires a relationship with every man, woman, boy, and girl. Through this relationship with Jesus, we encounter a soul-filled life that experiences the genuine love, life, and liberty of God.

The question is, do you have a personal relationship with Jesus? Are you saved? Huh? Saved, you may ask? Yes, are you saved? Jesus came to earth for this primary reason. Jesus did not come to give us fancy Christmas speeches. He did not come to give us a juicy Christmas story. Jesus came to save and deliver us from sin. He paid our sin debt in full by taking on our place on Calvary. The blood of bulls and goats could not save us from the penalty, presence, and punishment of sin. Only Jesus could fulfill the righteous requirement of the law. Biblical history is given to us to show how much God loved humanity that He came looking for you and me. Having a relationship with Jesus is about believing and receiving Him as the only begotten Son of God, the Savior of the world, who is the only one qualified to save us from the eternal penalty of sin.

This is not about religion, but I'm advocating that you choose to have a personal relationship with Jesus Christ. I am asking, have you asked Jesus Christ to forgive your sins? If not, please take time to read the below scriptures and make a conscious decision to repent of your sins and accept Jesus Christ as your Lord and Savior by faith into your heart. Trust me; this will be the best and greatest decision of your life. You will experience the eternal, unconditional love of God and experience the abundant life growing in the grace and knowledge of our Lord and Savior, Jesus Christ.

> *For all have sinned and fall short of the glory of God.* **Romans 3:23 (NIV)**

> *But God demonstrates His own love toward us, in that while we were still sinners, Christ died for us.* **Romans 5:8 (NKJV)**

> *For the wages of sin is death, but the gift of God is eternal life in Christ Jesus our Lord.* **Romans 6:23 (ESV)**

*But what does it say? "The word is near you,
in your mouth and in your heart" (that is, the
word of faith which we preach): that if you
confess with your mouth the Lord Jesus and
believe in your heart that God has raised Him
from the dead, you will be saved. For with the
heart one believes unto righteousness, and with
the mouth confession is made unto salvation.*
Romans 10:8–10 (NKJV)

*For "whoever calls on the name of the Lord
shall be saved."* **Romans 10:13 (NKJV)**

If you are ready to receive God's gift of salvation,
just speak these words to Jesus and give your life to Him:
"Dear Lord Jesus, I am a sinner. I ask for Your forgiveness
of my sins. I confess with my mouth and believe in my
heart by faith that You are the Son of God; I believe You
came to earth, lived, died on Calvary, and rose again so
that I could be given the right to be a child of God. I
believe in my heart that You are my Lord and Savior. I
commit my life to You. I believe you have set me free
from every evil work and Satan the evil one. I belong to
You, Lord Jesus. Use me for Your glory. Thank You, Lord
Jesus, for saving me. Amen.

Praise the Lord! Welcome to the Family of God!

As you start your walk in the faith, I encourage you to
pray and ask God to lead you to a Bible-believing local
church family. I also encourage you to start your Bible

reading in the New Testament with the Gospels: Matthew, Mark, Luke, and John. These four books of the New Testament share the story of Jesus. They explain who Jesus is, why He came, and why we need Him. For other passages on dealing with life and living by the wisdom of God, please read the book of Psalm and Proverbs. These two books are loaded with power-packed scriptures that will bless your heart and remind you of the care, love, peace, and sovereignty of God in your life. Just for starters, below are a few Bible readings to remind you of God's blessed assurance and presence in your life. Remember to take it one day at a time, keep your armor on (read Ephesians 6:10–20), and continue living the soulful life through Jesus Christ our Lord.

> A Psalm of David.
> *The Lord is my shepherd; I shall not want.*
> *He makes me to lie down in green pastures;*
> *He leads me beside the still waters. He*
> *restores my soul; He leads me in the paths*
> *of righteousness for His name's sake. Yea,*
> *though I walk through the valley of the*
> *shadow of death, I will fear no evil; for You*
> *are with me; Your rod and Your staff, they*
> *comfort me. You prepare a table before me*
> *in the presence of my enemies; You anoint*
> *my head with oil; My cup runs over.6 Surely*
> *goodness and mercy shall follow me all the*
> *days of my life; and I will dwell in the house*
> *of the Lord forever.* **Psalm 23 (NKJV)**

He who dwells in the secret place of the Most High shall abide under the shadow of the Almighty. I will say of the Lord, "He is my refuge and my fortress; My God, in Him I will trust." Surely He shall deliver you from the snare of the fowler and from the perilous pestilence. He shall cover you with His feathers, And under His wings you shall take refuge; His truth shall be your shield and buckler. You shall not be afraid of the terror by night, nor of the arrow that flies by day, nor of the pestilence that walks in darkness, nor of the destruction that lays waste at noonday. A thousand may fall at your side, and ten thousand at your right hand; but it shall not come near you. **Psalm 91:1–7 (NKJV)**

Trust in the Lord with all your heart, and lean not on your own understanding; in all your ways acknowledge Him, and He shall direct your paths. **Proverbs 3:5–6 (NKJV)**

For God so loved the world that He gave His only begotten Son, that whoever believes in Him should not perish but have everlasting life. For God did not send His Son into the world to condemn the world, but that the world through Him might be saved. **John 3:16–17 (NKJV)**

My sheep hear My voice, and I know them, and they follow Me. And I give them eternal life, and they shall never perish; neither shall anyone snatch them out of My hand. My

Father, who has given them to Me, is greater than all; and no one is able to snatch them out of My Father's hand. I   and My Father are one. **John 10:27–30 (NKJV)**

If you love Me, keep My commandments. And I will pray the Father, and He will give you another Helper, that He may abide with you forever—the Spirit of truth, whom the world cannot receive, because it neither sees Him nor knows Him; but you know Him, for He dwells with you and will be in you. I will not leave you orphans; I will come to you. **John 14:15–18 (NKJV)**

These things I have spoken to you, that in Me you may have peace. In the world you will have tribulation; but be of good cheer, I have overcome the world. **John 16:33 (NKJV)**

I do not pray that You should take them out of the world, but that You should keep them from the evil one. They are not of the world, just as I am not of the world. Sanctify them by Your truth. Your word is truth. As You sent Me into the world, I also have sent them into the world. And for their sakes I sanctify Myself, that they also may be sanctified by the truth. **John 17:15–19 (NKJV)**

Bibliography

Aesop. *Aesop's Fable: The Hare and The Tortoise.*
Translated by V. S. Vernon Jones. Amazon
Classics Edition, Kindle, 2019.

Bradbury, William B. "Solid Rock," In *Devotional
Hymn and Tune Book.* 620. New York: American Baptist
Publication Society, 1864.

Brown, Jeannine K. Brown, Matthew. *The Baker
Illustrated Bible Commentary.* 978–980. Edited   by
Gary M. Burge and Andrew E. Hill Grand Rapids: Baker
Books, 2012.

Denslow, W. W. Denslow, *Denslow's Humpty Dumpty.*
Illustrated by Osama Nasr. Amazon Services LLC,
Kindle, 2017.

Halliwell-Phillips, James. *The Three Little Pig. A Classic
Tale from Hayes Mountain.* Hayes   Mountain LLC,
Kindle, 2019.

Maurois, Andre. *The Life of Sir Alexander Fleming.*
135–157. Translated by Gerard Hopkins.   Mitcham:
Penguin Books, 1963.

*Morris, Grace. Morris, What to Watch, "Undercover Big
Boss' — ITV release date, premise, trailer, and all you
need to know" July 27, 2021.https://www.whattowatch.*

com/watching-guides/undercover-big-boss-itv-release-date-premise-trailer-and-all-you-need-to-know.

Schuller, Robert A. What Happens to Good People When Bad Things Happen. 12. Grand Rapids: Fleming H. Revell, 1995.

About the Author

Allen J. Shuler, Jr., was born and raised in Macon, GA. Allen received Jesus Christ as Lord and Savior and water baptism at the age of nine. He later answered the calling of God upon his life to preach the gospel of Jesus Christ. For over thirty years, Allen has faithfully served the Lord Jesus Christ, members of the military, their families, local Christian churches and communities throughout the United States, East Asia, Europe, and Southwest Asia. Allen currently serves as a Chaplain for Wesley Willows Senior Living Community. Allen and his wife, Constance, reside in Illinois. They are blessed with seven adult children and eleven grandchildren.

Allen graduated from Jones County High School. He actively participated in band and sports. After high school, Allen successfully walked-on the football team at the University of Georgia. After a two-year run of collegiate football, Allen changed direction and he enlisted into the US Army. This surprisingly unscripted turn in Allen's life gave him the opportunity to serve across North America and throughout the world. Allen says, "joining the military was one of my best decisions!" After twenty-five years, Allen honorably retired from the US Army, ending his military service as a Chief Warrant Officer-Four. Allen has received numerous awards for his military and community service to include the prestigious Legion of Merit, Bronze Star (w/oak leaf cluster) and Distinguished Order of Saint Martin for exceptional leadership and meritorious service to our nation. Allen earned a Bachelor of Science in Public Management from Austin Peay State University. He earned Master degrees in Divinity and Theological Studies from Liberty University John W. Rawlings School of Divinity. Most recently Allen served as the pastor of Olivet Baptist Church in Rock Island, IL. He served as a member of the Wood River Baptist District Association; the Friendship Manor Senior Living Continuing Care Development Committee; the Rock Island NAACP Religious Affairs Committee; the Unity Point Hospital Clinical Pastoral Education (CPE) Advisory Committee; and Associate Youth Program Specialist for Youth Hope Community Center in Moline, Il.

Beyond any earthly success, Allen and his wife, Constance, are compassionate visionary leaders who love encouraging and teaching all people to become fruitful disciples of Jesus Christ. They love people and deeply believe every man, woman, and child can have a prosperous soul-filled life: a life that lives as Jesus lives; loves like Jesus loves; and serve others like Jesus teaches us to serve.

CPSIA information can be obtained
at www.ICGtesting.com
Printed in the USA
LVHW041926240422
717100LV00012B/257